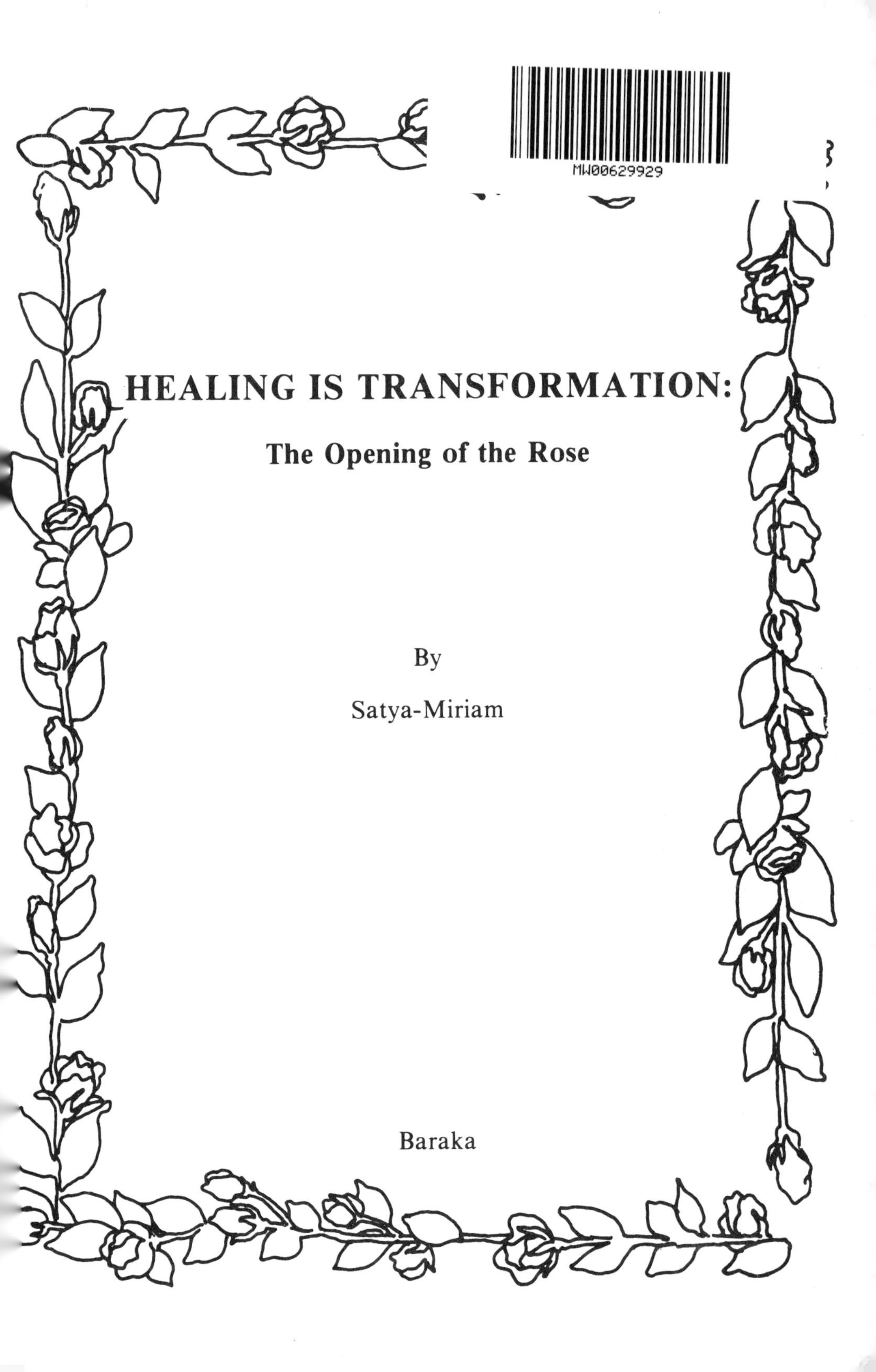

HEALING IS TRANSFORMATION:

The Opening of the Rose

By

Satya-Miriam

Baraka

Baraka Books, Ltd.
453 Greenwich St.
New York, New York

Printed in the U.S.A. by

Baraka Press, Inc.

ISBN No. 0-88238-987-4
Library of Congress Card Catalog No. 78-64491

Dedicated to the Reader:

In Acknowledgement of who you really are

TABLE OF CONTENTS

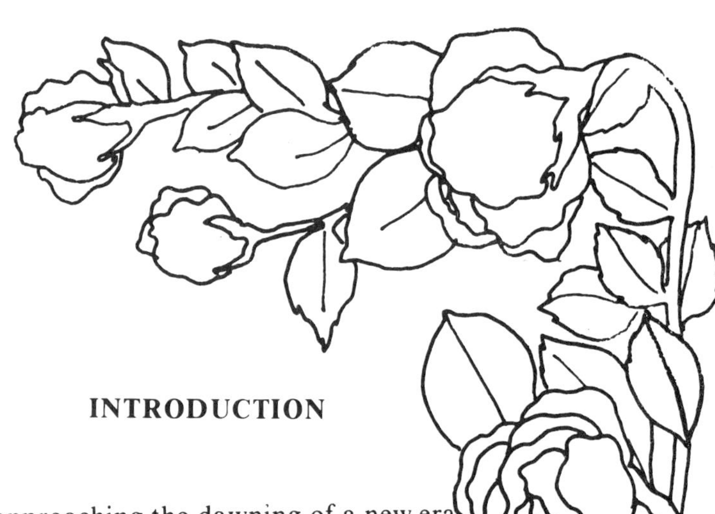

INTRODUCTION

We are approaching the dawning of a new era in planetary and human evolution. Our consciousness is opening to the presence of spiritual love. This is not a superfluous shift, but rather one that is necessary for our survival. It will help us regain our sight, and perhaps then we will understand that our spiritual nature and our material conditions, including the health of our bodies, are an expression of the same truth.

I hope that this book will function as an aid during this time of awakening. We are experiencing rapid transformation and because of this we must continually learn how to heal our bodies, minds and hearts. All that is really demanded of us is that we stay true to ourselves, and yet often that is the hardest thing to do. It would be good to view this book as an ally which has healing power all of its own, and has come to help heal you. How the power and magic of the book works with you depends on how you work with it. It is well to treat the ideas presented with respect. These ideas may have an effect which is more far-reaching than your rational mind, although it is good to use your mind to absorb the information presented. The book has the capacity to act as a catalyst for your healing process. No one can give anyone all the answers about how to heal themselves, for at the core of healing lies a deep mystery that is to be respected. It is the mystery of transformation and regeneration and is different for each person. It is the mystery of balance and harmony, and at the core of this mystery lies the universal heart.

Be gentle with yourself when using this book. Do not expect the impossible. If this book helps you to be kinder to yourself, then a great victory has been won. Above all, don't let this book fill the mind with more should's and should nots; rather let it give you more space simply to be and let it guide you to your own understanding of your healing process.

Although I use the word "you" in this book, I do not feel that I know anymore truth than the reader. For me, the word "you" and "we" are the same. I have chosen to use the word "you" often throughout the text so that the material would reach you, the individual reader, more personally.

I do not claim to be a healer. I only wish to share with you some of my perceptions about healing processes. The book by no means attempts to displace or discredit traditional medical healing methods. It speaks at a different angle, but does not take argument here with the medical profession.

The most consistent thing I've learned and experienced through the work I do is the continual confirmation of God's love and mercy for us. This extends to all facets of our lives.

It is through faith, and more important love, that enables me to do this work. I pray that we all grow in faith and love. This is my deepest concern.

We must learn how to love ourselves and each other. This is the foundation upon which the new age will be built. This is the only way we can experience our healing on all levels.

We will be healed through the golden crown of heaven. This is my deepest certainty.

I have come to understand deeply that the love and mercy of God JUST IS. It is we who put the blinders on so that we cannot experience it. I hope this book will help to tear away at some of the blinders, as we open ourselves to our own healing process, and blossom like a rose in our hearts.

CHAPTER I
HEALING AS A PROCESS

The Opening of the Rose

If we allow ourselves to accept the fact that healing is a process, we can allow ourselves to experience our own healing. The healing process is similar to the way a Rose opens it is a gentle unfolding which leads us to who we really are.

As we encourage ourselves to be who we really are, we move into a vibration and a rhythym which is a harmonious expression of our being. As we properly align ourselves, our physical and mental health increase.

To experience this opening of the Rose is to experience the opening of Love in our Hearts. If we participate responsibly in our healing process we insure the inevitability of our transformation. We move from limitation and sorrow to limitless Love.

Healing means to be whole. To become whole means to become holy. To become holy means to be who we really are. When we allow ourselves to be who we really are, the cells in our bodies will sing in harmony and joy. The cells in our bodies can only be healed through limitless Love which is the Light.

Intuition

There are certain prerequisites to the healing process. The first is to know that the potential for healing is within, and second, to know that you have the capacity to discern what is necessary for your healing transformation.

This discernment is possible through your intuition. Intuition means inner hearing. It is the ability to go beyond your rational mind to listen to the deepest and truest part of yourself. Intuition is being in an attitude of receptive listening.

You need to allow quiet for this aspect of your healing process. You need time to relax and let the noise of the world and your mental concepts dissolve. It is often very hard for you to give yourself permission to do this. By listening to your intuition you are basically giving yourself permission to be. This is a brave act.

Developing workable intuition is similar to tuning into a new radio station. It requires attention to find out where it is on the dial. If you are new at this it is best to lie down and let your cares, worries and entanglements fall away till all that you see is the sunlight. Feel yourself floating gently above the clouds in the sunlight. Ask yourself what it is you need to do to be well.

The guidance you might receive from yourself can be as practical as changing a job, or as subtle as changing a mental attitude.

During the course of the day you do not always have time to relax and tune into yourself. So in addition to allowing yourself time to be quiet and listen, you must also learn to follow your intuition in an instinctual spontaneous way. It is possible to be and to act in accord with yourself in all situations which life presents to you without judging yourself or others. Following your intuition is really an act of faith: it is trusting the process of healing.

The most important thing to do is to begin to make this link to yourself by tuning into a very subtle part of your being as well as trusting your experience. By giving ourselves the psychic space to be at ease with our experience without constantly judging yourself will come the reality of your healing.

Dreams in Healing

Another way you can receive inner guidance is through the abundant Kingdom of your dreams. It is not hard to remember your dreams. All you need to do is to tell yourself before you go to bed that you will remember your dreams and to keep a notebook or tape recorder nearby to record them as soon as you awake. After a couple of months of doing this, you will be able to record your dreams for the rest of your life. When you remember and appreciate your dreams you can be given great gifts from them.

I often have dreams that give me very specific guidance for what I need to do to heal myself. I dream about kinds of vitamins or foods I need, in which ways I'm out of balance in my relationships, and receive information about the work I do.

The most helpful dreams are those which enable us to see more clearly. These dreams are often of a prophetic nature. Sometimes it is necessary to ask until you receive what you need help with. Dreams like this are usually a statement of what is really going on in a particular situation. Here are three examples of this type of dream.

A friend of mine and I were both clearing out a lot of hurtful patterns in our lives. One night, when I was staying over at her house, we each had similar dreams. I dreamt I was crossing the ocean and had arrived at Newfoundland. My friend, in the room next to me, dreamt she was meeting Christopher Columbus, who was congratulating her on her move to the New World.

This same friend also dreamt about a specific new age center of healing. A man wearing golden feathers was sweeping them around her and healing her. The very next day she met, for the first time the people who ran the center. When she told them the dream she had they were very encouraged to continue their work.

I once heard a woman spiritual teacher speak about a dream she had about the time she was building a spiritual center. In the dream she was wearing a white gown which was soiled. As she thought about the dream she came to the realization that she was too interested in her gain in the situation and was able to let go of that self-interest.

Dreams and symbols are interwoven and sometimes we must do some work to uncover the message of our dreams. A man came to me with a dream about his knees feeling weak. During the consultation we discovered that he wasn't getting his needs met, and that the word "knees" in the dream meant the word "needs".

Besides interpreting them, you can also work creatively with the symbols which arise from your dreams. A woman who was taking over a group I was leading had a frightening experience in a dream of a monster chasing her. I asked her to draw the monster and as she did she began to become friends with it. She brought the drawing of the monster to the group, and it now looked like a magical ally. She was able to transmute her fear through work with her dream.

Dreams can also show us how we want things to be. Sometimes it is appropriate to work on fulfilling the wishes which become disclosed through our dreams. Sometimes it is not appropriate, and so we must discriminate between which dreams to follow and which to leave behind.

Dreams can also be a way for a person to discharge negativity and fear. This is most certain to happen when we are going through a lot of change in our lives. It is as if the old stuff is being cleared out, so that the new may occur in our lives.

Many people receive spiritual instruction and initiation in

their dreams. In these situations, the subtle body of the master and the disciple meet.

The Light in Healing

Because we live in a world of so much darkness and fear we must learn how to work with the Light. We are transformed through the Light in our healing process. In order to understand the importance of the Light in healing, we need to have faith that the power and majesty of the Light of God is so great that it can heal whatever is necessary, whether it be on physical, mental or emotional levels. It is through that Light that Jesus the man became the Christ, or the Annointed One. It is through its power that he healed so many on earth. It is through the power of the Light that we are continually resurrected, or made new. The story of the transformative power of the Light is no one else's story but our own. We are being transformed into what we already are. This is our story of the Light. This is the story of our Healing.

The most basic and necessary way for us to work in accord with the Light of God is simply to love it. As we become absorbed in our love for it, we merge into it. We become beings of Light.

If we pray with genuine Love to experience the purity of the Light within us (and yet independent of us for its existence), we immediately tap a powerful source of strength and mercy which is love itself. This is the beginning of the removal of barriers. If we pray to the Light without this genuine Love for its nature but only for what we hope to gain, we distort the purpose of our transformative quest.

We can see prayer as an offering of ourselves to the Light of God. But we must understand that in this offering is contained our reward, for we are gaining our very essence, our very selves. This type of prayer is communion, and it is through this type of prayer that we are becoming our own beloved. This is the opening of the Rose and this is the seed of our transformation. With this spirit of prayer we can then ask for our needs to be met. We can ask for physical healing with the firm belief that it is more than possible. We can pray for strength and clarity, and to be in accord with the will of God. All of this will be given to us. We are the inheritors of the Kingdom.

By prayer, by asking, we are actually invoking the necessary change in our lives. We are in effect calling forth the power of the word. The power of the word is very monumental, and it is well to contemplate John 1:5. "In the beginning was the Word, and the Word was with God, and the Word was God. He was in the beginning with God; all things were made through him, and without him was not anything made that was made. In him was Life, and the life was the light of men. The Light shines in the darkness; and the darkness has not overcome it."

The power of the Word therefore has the capacity to invoke the Light of God in healing. This is the spark that ignites the fire of our healing process. This aspect of prayer, or invocation, is also dependent on what we put into it. What we put into it is dependent on whether we feel we deserve to live or not. We are not passive participants in prayer; we must continually make a stand for ourselves and our right to be. We must give ourselves permission to be so that we can truly benefit in prayer. A man came to me the other day for a consultation and told me all the things that were going wrong in his life as well as everything he was doing wrong. He thought if only he could do this or that right he would be able to think well of himself. I suggested to him that what was basically necessary was to give himself permission to be alive, apart from any external situation or relationship. I asked him to imagine himself living all the time with this feeling of having permission to be alive. It is time for all of us to give ourselves permission to be alive.

With this gift, which we bestow upon ourselves, we can pray for what we feel we need at the time. It can be for physical and emotional well-being, prosperity and clarification, as well as to ask for purity to serve the Light of God so that it can manifest on Earth. As we pray for our needs to be met and to align ourselves with the will of God we offer it all to God. Through the power of the Word in prayer and the sincerity in our hearts, events happen in our outer as well as our inner life to push and guide us toward our goal.

As these events take place, we refine and discover more of what we really need and who we really are. As we begin to rediscover our being we allow ourselves to be guided more and more by the Light. This is the process of healing with the Light.

If we allow the Light to burn off the dross from the gold to regain our spiritual sight. In turning to the Light, we turn to ourselves. To turn to the Light is to turn to who we really are.

To ask the Light to heal our infirmities is a beautiful task. By doing this we are taking another step to being ministers of Light: by asking we cannot help but receive and by receiving Love-Light we cannot help but share this with others.

To share it with others is to receive the Love-Light throughout our lives.

To ask the Light to dispel fear so that we can have faith and be healed is to overcome fear.

To ask the Light to teach us and to guide us is to truly love.

To ask the Light to heal us is to overcome our limited desires for the Love of God, who is our own heart.

By receiving the Mercy of the Light, we are opening the portals of Mercy to all who are ready to partake.

CHAPTER II
THE OPENING OF THE ROSE

Listening and Talking To Our Bodies

The process of opening of the Rose requires a beautiful caring for ourselves as well as others. This kind of caring for ourselves is not a passive endeavor, but rather requires a subtle active awareness of how our body and psyche work together. The symptoms of disease can be seen as a physical or emotional expression. If we allow ourselves the psychic space to understand what needs to be expressed, it is possible the symptoms as well as their cause can be alleviated.

All cells in the body have consciousness and we can communicate with parts of our body or the whole of our body. The first aspect of this form of communication is to learn to listen to the messages which our body communicates to us. The second aspect of this form of communication is to respect all of these messages, the painful as well as the pleasurable ones.

The organs of your body can act as guidelines to let you know what is going on with your psyche. This means that the functions of your body are connected. The digestive system, for example, also reflects the way you digest psychically. The breasts concern self-nourishment. The womb, ovaries or male sexual organs indicate creative generative energy. The sexual organs also symbolize an openness to life. The malfunction of the lymphatic system may mean you have not protected yourself adequately. Kidneys are often connected with sexual fear, or fear of letting go in general. To have your kidneys functioning well means you are flowing with your life. Wherever you have fear, resentment, or don't think well enough of yourself, it is likely to show on the human body. Ultimately, the physical and metaphysical are the same.

What's more important than these general guideposts given about the few parts of the body is learning how to tune into yourself so that you can listen and talk with your body. Each person's story is unique, and so the best person to understand what is going on with you is you. All that is necessary to do this is to relax, be quiet, and take your consciousness to the part of the body that is causing your discomfort and ask it what is wrong or what it/you need in order to feel better. Then allow yourself to listen with the awareness that you can tune into the consciousness of that particular part of your body/psyche. This part of the healing process is important because physical symptoms must be worked with and honored rather than disregarded or disdained. So it is most important for you not to reject your pain, but allow it to guide you towards greater self-knowledge and healing. If you tune into a part of your body that seems to be saying, "I hate you" or "I don't want to live" you may suddenly see where this feeling came from in your past. Cells have consciousness, as we said before, and they also store memories. The memories could be of unhappy incidents or feelings, or even of a trauma that occurred yesterday. The first thing to be done is to allow yourself to experience whatever it is that you have been holding in your body. So discharge is an important part of our healing process. That usually means to allow yourself to feel your pain instead of discrediting or rejecting your experience because it is uncomfortable. This acceptance of your denied and rejected experience is a vital part of the healing process. As you accept and re-experience the impressions holding in your physical or emotional body, you begin to eliminate them.

Elimination and Regeneration

Elimination, or discharge, is vital to our physical, emotional, and mental bodies. We have all unconsciously absorbed negative thoughts that poisoned us for years. So the need for elimination, which really means to consciously experience the pain and negativity and then to let go of it is very great. If we deny ourselves this right, we will not be able to experience the nature of the Rose, or our own Beauty.

To be able to experience whatever it is we are holding in our bodies and to let go of this enables us to make way for the new. Sometimes, before you undergo a big change you go through an intense period of discomfort where you are eliminating the old so that there can be an opening for the new.

As great as is the need for elimination, so is the need for regeneration or rebuilding. So, for example, if we take our consciousness to the part of the body that said "I hate you" we may continue and ask it, "What do you need in order to feel better about yourself?" and we must once again listen receptively to what our body has to say. Here, we are beginning to enter into the creative act of healing. It could be that the simple message we receive from our body is, "I need you to love me more." Here, once again, we are encountered with the truth that we have to love ourselves. We could also receive a more specific message about how we go about loving ourselves. Perhaps guidance like "I need you to take care of me better by listening to me when I'm tired or need to be soothed." Perhaps it is a specific thing to do, such as a change of job or relationship.

In any case, this part of the healing process we can label receptive listening. This means we are able to listen to ourselves, including a particular part of the body, with love and respect. It is important not to deny or reject our pain or discomfort, but rather to use our pain as a guide and a friend. As well as listening to our body, we can also talk with our body. It is an important phase of healing, for here we can give our body mental directive. We can tell our body to relax, repair and regenerate. We can take the message our body has given us and work with it.

For instance, supposing when we ask our body what it needs to do to get better it says, "I need to leave the job I'm doing." But we're not able to leave the job for another year because of important committments. We can say to our body, "I can't leave this job yet but I can take more time doing enjoyable regenerating activities." What we are doing when we are talking to our bodies is sending love to ourselves. Again, it is of no use to talk to our body if we cannot love ourselves.

Thoughts in Healing

In order to be well, we need to think of ourselves as being well. A healer once said that "energy follows thought" and this is entirely true.

Our thoughts are vehicles in which the healing energy is transmitted. Swami Sivananda, in the book "Thought Power",* says:

> Thoughts are living things. A thought is as much solid as a piece of stone . . .
>
> Thought has got tremendous power. Thought can heal diseases. Thought can transform the mentality of persons. Thought can do anything. It can work wonders . . .
>
> "Every impulse of the mind, every thought is conveyed to the cells. They are greatly influenced by the varying conditions or states of the mind. If there are confusion, depression and other negative emotions

*Divine Life Society, P.O. Sivanandanagar Dt. Jehar, Garhual U.P., Himalayas, India. Used here with permission of the General Secretary.

> or thoughts in the mind, they are telegraphically transmitted through the nerves to every cell in the body. The soldier-cells become panic-stricken. They are weakened. They are not able to perform their functions properly.

The way we use thoughts is one of the most essential ingredients in how we heal ourselves and how we are collectively healed. We need to see very clearly the effect of our thoughts on our physical environment as well as on the more subtle dealings in our life. We need to realize that the axiom, "as we think, so we shall be" is a true one.

If we think well of ourselves we will be well, and if we think harshly of ourselves, our life conditions will be harsh.

If we use our thoughts creatively and visualize them surrounded and completely permeated with light, we can heal ourselves. We have to be able to clearly see or visualize the cells and tissues of our body healed. We have to be able to creatively see or visualize the planet as radiating light and peace. All of this is possible if we think well of ourselves and others. This is the power of thought.

To creatively see with our thoughts is to visualize. To visualize is to hold in the mind's eye the pattern of the future. We can visualize ourselves healthy, the cells in our body being filled with Light. We can also visualize how we want our lives to be.

The acceptance of the power of thought in healing is still in its infancy stages in our culture. As our minds become clearer, as we align ourselves more with the will of the Lord, our thoughts will take on the quality of crystal. We will be able, through our thoughts, to transmit and reflect the Light in healing.

To work with creative visualization, we must envision ourselves as seekers of the Light of the Holy Grail. Then we must allow ourselves to live our truest vision. In this way we will become ourselves and also uplift the planet.

I have experienced the power of thought in healing many times, both with myself and in people with whom I have done consultations. The body wants to be well and if it is given mental directive and/or encouragement, to this effect, it will begin to readjust itself in the direction of health or wholeness. One thing I do when people come to me for consultations is to surround them with Light and see them totally well. What this does basically is to give the cells in the body a chance to absorb and detoxify wastes. Then I tune into the specific problem and work with the person on the causes of a particular disharmony. This helps to readjust the person's energy so that more vitality can flow through the person. At the end of the session we both envision the person healthy and in accord with him/herself and his/her environment. The power of visualizing helps the cells readjust to a more harmonious frequency where healing can be possible.

To visualize ourselves well is something that must be done frequently, once or twice a day, in a relaxed state of mind. It can be done in a very specific way, i.e., one organ or functioning system in the body, or it can be done in a more general way. The mind needs to be clear for this work and the body needs to be relaxed so that the necessary changes can take place.

Breath in Healing

The great Sufi master Hazrat Inayat Khan said about breath:

> "A healer must know in the first place that breath is the very life, that breath is the giver of life, and that breath is the bringer of life."

When we inhale, we bring the element of air into our bodies and recharge our system. When we exhale we let out the toxins which become revitalized through the air. Breathing is the link

* Reprinted with permission of the International Headquarters of the Sufi Movement, Geneva, from THE DEVELOPMENT OF SPIRITUAL HEALING, published by Sufi Publishing Company Ltd., UK ISBN: 0.900217.15.4 c International Headquarters of the Sufi Movement, Geneva, 1962.

of the soul to the body. As we breathe, we take in life from the Holy Body, and we offer life to the Holy Body. Because breath is the giver of life, we can also heal ourselves through the breath and the power of thought and visualization. Here is an exercise to do to allow the breath to heal you: Relax and allow yourself to breathe in life and light. Visualize it filling your body with the life-giving energy of Christ or another divine being of Light. Allow your infirmities to be dissolved by this divine energy which is the bestower of all life. As you exhale let all of your fears and negativities go out of you and be reabsorbed by the Light.

Continue to inhale the life-giving energy of God and let it fill and heal all of your body. Continue to exhale all of your pain and tension and disappointment.

Realize that you are working with the Light through your breath and that you are being given renewed life by the creative spirit of God. As you inhale let the Light dissolve all of the concepts and rigidity that keep you from being yourself. As you exhale, feel yourself expanding beyond your concepts, fears and limitations.

As you inhale, allow yourself to be one with the essence of the Light. Continue to feel yourself being uplifted and expanded.

As you exhale, feel that you are exhaling pure Light that merges into pure Light.]

Color in Healing

If the subtle form of the Light is capable of healing our infirmities, then color, which is a part of Light, also is capable of healing. We live in a world of color and Light and yet most of the time we are not conscious of its movement in us. Color and Light are fine vibrations or waves of subtle energy which can cleanse and harmonize the cells in our body. One of the ways in which this is done is by establishing a harmonic rhythm within the cells. When the cells and organs vibrate in harmony, vitality and health are possible.

Color as a force in healing works in many beautiful ways. Just as we take in food to restore our bodies, so we can take in and allow color to heal us. Most people have a basic color tone that is an expression of their being. At different times in our lives we need various colors of the spectrum to help us re-balance and to re-harmonize.

The only way the color rays of the healing Light can work for us is through our profound respect. We get to know the healing colors through our sincere desire to do so. Our rational minds can understand that color is a wave vibration and that a vibration is capable of transmitting energy. But our love and respect for the colors must co-exist with our love for the Light.

Here is an exercise to allow you to intuitively get to know the colors and their effects on you. It is best to have someone read this exercise slowly and softly to you.

Allow yourself to relax and be comfortable. Slowly let the cares of the day go. Now see yourself walking in a pine forest. You are walking barefoot, for it is a very warm summer day. You can feel the soft pine needles form a cushion under your feet. Soon you come to an opening: a circle of pine trees. You enter the circle and feel the golden radiance of the sun. Allow yourself to stand there quietly for a few minutes and then silently invoke the Golden Ray Vibration and see it surrounding you and at the same time filling your body. Ask it to heal you in the way that is most appropriate for you and keep visualizing yourself becoming one with the Golden Ray Vibration. Ask it whether it has anything to teach you and allow yourself to be in total accord with this Vibration.

When the Golden Ray Vibration leaves, see yourself surrounded and permeated by all the color ray vibrations of the rainbow and beyond. Let all these beautiful colors totally surround you, tones that are both soothing, subtle and brilliant, colors that are able to totally renew and recharge all the cells of your physical body as well as your emotional and mental bodies. Colors that are of the Great White Light and that can dispel every fearful negative thought, every devitalized congested area of the body. See all of the colors vibrating in and around your body so that all of the cells of your body start moving to their own harmonious rhythm. Allow yourself to feel these colors both surrounding you and permeating you for a few more minutes.

*

Now just allow yourself to be back in the circle of pine trees. Ask and visualize the Red Ray color surrounding you and permeating you. Feel this color flowing through your bloodstream, giving you new vitality and courage. Red is the Ray Vibration to re-energize you and re-vitalize you. It is good for diseases like anemia.

**

Ask the Pink Ray to be with you and visualize it surrounding and interpenetrating your body. Feel yourself being one with this gentle Pink Ray Vibration and allow yourself to experience universal love and mercy through this ray vibration. Let this universal love and mercy heal you now.

*

Invoke the radiance of the Orange Ray Vibration to be with you. Visualize the Orange Ray Vibration revitalizing your glandular and sexual system. Feel your creative, generative energy revitalized by the Orange Color Ray.*

Now invoke the Yellow Ray Vibration to completely surround and permeate you. Feel it softening up old resistances and dispelling fear. Feel it uplifting your mind to a positive mental outlook.

*

Again, be aware of being in the center of the circle of pines. Feel the warmth of the sun and look at the color ray vibration green from the pine trees. Begin to be at peace and harmony with the green and see yourself surrounded and permeated with green. Let the Green Ray Vibration restore balance, peace and harmony to your entire system. Visualize yourself leading a life of balance and restoration.

*

Now let the color blue surround and fill your body. Blue is the soothing color ray. It is good for headaches, arthritis, and general tension. Allow yourself to be totally soothed and gently healed by the wonderful color blue.

*

Ask the Purple Ray Vibration to be with you and to totally surround your body. Feel the spiritual sustenance and peace of this ray as this color surrounds you.

*

Now ask the Silver Ray to be with you and feel yourself being transformed by the Silver Ray Vibration. See yourself being lifted by the stars and feel yourself totally surrounded by the Silver Ray .

Continue to feel lighter and lighter. Let the color ray vibration of silver change into brilliant white light. Feel yourself being the white light. Feel the white light as love. Feel yourself as being total Love.

***

The color rays really come where they are needed and work how they are needed. Sometimes two or more come together, sometimes only one is necessary. It is best to ask your body, or a specific organ or system in your body, what color is necessary to help you be healed. If you listen, you will hear. As you hear, the colors will be working with you.

The color ray vibrations as a manifestation of the Light are with us always. As we become increasingly aware of their presence, we can appreciate more and more their beauty and transformative power.

*

I would like to share with you what a man who took a workshop I taught on healing shared with me. He was an Englishman and at one point in his life he was very sick in London. Nothing was helping him. One night he felt the presence of all of the color ray vibrations in three circles around him, along with the presence of Jesus. They stayed with him all night and in the morning he was completely healed.

The Need for Discrimination in Healing

Part of your healing process is involved in being able to discriminate. Appropriately what is necessary for you and what is unnecessary for you are issues which confront you continually. Sometimes forebearance, or the ability to tolerate situations is necessary; at other times, assertion is necessary. What kinds of foods to eat, what kind of company to keep, what kind of exercise to get are all things that require discrimination. Discrimination is an important way to reduce stress-filled situations. Knowing what people to engage in extended conversation in your work is important. You need discrimination when you seek medical help. You need discrimination to know what healer is really truthful and effective and helpful. If you go to an astrologer or healer or psychic or physician who is negative or who does not have a pure mine, you are bound to be influenced in a way that is not helpful to you. Here, discrimination and intuition walk hand in hand to guide us. You need to know what dreams are appropriate to follow, and what dreams are appropriate to disregard. You can ask for guidance within whenever it is necessary. You can be sure that you will act with appropriate ease if you take the time to credit yourself with intuitively knowing what is right for you.

The Healing Crisis

There is another part of the healing process that it is important to say a few words about. It is called by homeopaths a "healing crisis" and it refers to the time in the healing process that different symptoms and the cause for the symptoms surface to a greater intensity, either in the body or in the psyche or in both. This part of the healing process is unavoidable, and should be seen as a blessing. It is the intense part of the eliminative process and although it is uncomfortable, it is healing nonetheless. You cannot have the illusion that your pains will be magically taken away. Rather, you need to allow this cleansing and surfacing of the causes of your symptoms to occur. The healing crisis will happen many times during your life, so you must not expect to experience it only once. It must be understood that at this point in our evolutionary development, when so much cleansing is taking place on the planet, that a healing crisis is a very intrinsic part of everyone's healing process. For this to be effectively carried out, we must be very strong and treat ourselves with kindness.

The healing crisis takes different forms. The body could be discharging in order to purify itself. Negative and fearful emotions may fill your mind so that you cannot think of anything else for a few days. Often these fears and negativities are the thought forms that are the seed of physical disease.

Whatever form it takes, repeated healing crises in either a relatively mild or stronger form, are bound to occur if you are to be healed and you must learn to allow this to happen and stay turned towards the Light. You need to discriminate carefully during these times, and if you are actually getting worse you need to take another step for ourselves, for instance it is seeing a medical doctor, or taking a time of rest, etc.

While your healing's basic core is a mystery, you are not a passive participant in the process. You should be instead a conscious and active participant. The awareness of yourself exists within your body and it is time for you to evolve to the point of taking creative responsibility for yourself according to the precepts of the Masters. You must clearly understand that the power of healing lies within you. Healers only act as facilitator or catalysts so that a person's own healing energy can become activated. This is no different than what Christ meant when he said "The Kingdom of Heaven Lies Within."

This active form of self-healing will not only give you the power to heal yourself, it will also enable you to heal others. For if you can begin to experience the regenerative power being within yourself as well as outside yourself, you can genuinely love and serve others without making subtle demands. You don't have to worry about getting something you think you don't already have within yourself. This feeling of not having what we need within us gives rise to many false expectations which we place on ourselves, others, and all of the situations we encounter in life.

One of the main expectations that this false belief fosters is that a person or a particular situation (money, marriage, success) will give you the love or happiness you need. Even in your healing process you might go around searching for what you need, always relying on other's judgments. This does not mean not to rely or respect professional procedures and advice. Sometimes they are life saving. But still, it is your own healing process that you must, all and all, take responsibility for.

If we are not relying on other people's judgments, then we can try to inflict our opinions on someone else. Because we value everything except our own divinity we become prey to continual anxiety over the future, either asking for control from other people's judgments or trying to control others with our own judgments.

The truth is that we are all alright. That we are divine Love that is beyond intellectual understanding and that it is the blinders of pride and ignorance over our eyes that keep us fettered.

Making A Commitment to Your own Transformation

Another aspect of your healing process that needs clarification is making a commitment to your transformation. You must be able to change in whatever ways are necessary to allow you to follow your path and to bring you closer and closer to your true nature. The words "to heal" mean to become whole and this is what you must accept for yourself. The way to love yourself is to accept and to follow the deepest truest way for yourself. You must experience your living as your healing process. If you try to take short cuts you will become increasingly dishonest. As you become increasingly dishonest, it is hard not to hurt yourself and others. Also, when you become dishonest, you become increasingly ill at ease, and often this results in physical or emotional disease.

Your healing process is your life process and your life process is your healing process. Healing is not one isolated incident. So when I talk about healing, I am not only talking about a particular end to a specific pain or disease, although this no doubt does and should occur. I am talking about the process of transforming yourself.

Healing as a transformative experience means continual change. You should not hold on to illusions of the past that cannot work for you. You cannot hold on to illusions of the future that may not be suitable for you. All that you can do is to live fully the promise of the day and accept yourself and your right to exist on this planet.

The Function of Illness in our Lives

The reason for disease is often a mystery to me, but I have experienced that it can serve as a spiritual purification and transformation. The soul has taken on the garb of the body to experience its own divinity, and illness is often a disguised way for the soul to experience its own perfection. I will give you two examples of this from my own experience.

Once, a man wanted me to do a healing on him — he had pain due to pressure on a nerve. I felt intuitively that I should not do this, but he kept insisting. I tried, working against my intuition, but nothing happened. At this time of his life he was meditating intensely and he had asked his guru (before he asked me to help him) to either stop the pain or teach him a lesson from the experience. The pain continued and deepened and finally a few days later while he was meditating, he reached a part of his consciousness where he was able to transcend the pain. After he was able to reach this awareness, the pain that he had suffered disappeared. This incident taught me how the Lord teaches us, and in any attempt to heal ourselves or others, it is important to maintain humility and realize who it is who does the healing.

The other incident I want to share occurred in an on-going group I was facilitating entitled "The Opening of the Rose." One woman in the group, who was forty, came for the first two sessions and then became very ill for the remainder of the meetings of the group. Another woman in the group, who was also a friend of hers, went to her and did a Laying on of Hands. Soon after this, the woman who was ill broke into a fever which lasted for 24 hours and began her recovery. The woman came to the last meeting of the group and spoke to all the participants of the group about the need for purification, which is something she had thought of before her illness. Another interesting part of this story which the woman told me later was that her father, also at the age of forty, had a serious illness which changed his life radically for the better. If we truly trust our organism and its capacity for absolutely appropriate responses, we must also trust our illness.

Illness, when it is caught in its early stages, serves the important function of forcing us to understand ourselves better. In this case, the illness is a teacher which guides us to be in better harmony with who we really are. Illness helps us let go of illusions.

Whenever I feel physical discomfort I try to rest and allow myself to understand what I am doing that is out of alignment. Usually I am pursuing a course that is not quite in keeping with who I am, so I get sick to give myself a chance to reassess. When we view our physical symptoms as our friends, we have a good working tool to understand ourselves.

I am not saying that you should be attached to your illnesses and keep them unnecessarily. I am only saying that illness can be a necessary teacher for you if you allow yourself that experience. You may not always be able to understand the teachings of your illnesses immediately, so it is good to be patient with yourself.

Letting Go

An important aspect of your healing process is to be able to continually let go, as an act of opening to the power of grace and love and movement. It's an act of opening to the Rose.

Another important function in the process of letting go is allowing yourself to be made new each moment. In this newness is your healing potential and actualization. It is a continual dropping off of the encrustments that clutter you up from day to day so you can open to the beauty of all that you are. All that you really own is your experience. As you let go of daily situations and events, as you let go of the painful expectations of yourself and others, as you let go of your resentments and preconceptions, as you let go of your fear and sorrow, you allow yourself to be made new. In this newness is your freedom and your expansion.

You do not need to identify with every event and thought. You do need to identify with the fact that you are limitless love and light.

A simple thing to do every day is to relax and to alow yourself to let go of all the events and feelings of the day. To see yourself surrounded by the Light of the sun and being made new. Visualize all worries, resentments, and events falling away.

You must allow yourself to trust the process. Here you are at the heart of paradox; you must take total responsibility for your healing process and participate in the changes necessary, even if it is no more than a change of mental attitude, and you at the same time must constantly let go and surrender to your process.

CHAPTER III
SPIRITUAL LAW IN HEALING

All spiritual transmissions are precepts to live by. To follow spiritual law is to follow your true nature and to be established in a foundation within your own being that is unshakable. This simply means that there are ways of being that are important to follow so that you may be well. If you don't follow these laws of being, you will suffer until you reacquaint yourself with them.

Love the Lord Our God With All Your Heart

The direct law given to us in both the Old and New Testament is to Love the Lord thy God with all your hearts and souls and to Love your Neighbor as Yourself. When we are not able to love and honor our own divinity and the divinity within each other, many manifestations of inharmony occur. A disease like cancer is a mirror — here the cells in the body, instead of being in harmony and love with each other, destroy each other. To me, this is a microcosm of how we are taught to be competitive with each other and not to love God with all of our hearts. When we are able to honor and worship ourselves, we see love for each other and don't need to destroy ourselves by competing. An intellectual or skeptic might say that this is a simplistic vision. Yet simplicity can be a guiding post.

Ask and Ye Shall Receive

An important law in spiritual healing is "Ask and ye shall receive." This means you must say you want to be healed with the firm conviction that this will happen. Wanting to be healed sets in motion our healing process.

You should keep in mind also that disease is karmic, the result of past deeds that our soul-personality has led, and certain karmas cannot be erased immediately. They must be borne, so you may not have an immediate healing of your body. This does not mean that the body won't be healed, only that it is good not to focus only on that, but rather on how through such illnesses your soul is cleansed.

The Law of Acceptance

The Law of Acceptance simply means that you must first accept the reality of healing, not for just anybody, but for yourself, and then allow whatever changes necessary for your healing to occur. To accept the fact of your healing means to accept the fact that you are alive and that you deserve to live. To accept the possibility of your healing is to permit it to happen.

The Law of Attraction

The Law of Attraction means you attract the external situations in your life by your thoughts and feelings about yourself and what life has to offer you. You have to allow yourself to see clearly what you are attracting to yourself. Are you attracting health or disease, are you attracting loving relationships, are you attracting beautiful events in your life? Then you can consciously see what you want to attract to yourself and begin to make this a reality.

The Law of Accord

One way we can work with our healing process is to understand what is meant by the Law of Accord. The Law of Accord is specific for each of us because each of us is unique. When you are in accord with yourself and your environment, it is easier for you to experience physical and mental health. Your unique responsibility in learning how to heal yourself is to be aware of when you are in accord and when you are not and to be able to make appropriate readjustments in your life situations. The Law of Accord is therefore not a stagnant law, but involves movement in a rhythm that befits your particular vibration and sensitivity. Being in accord means living in a rhythmic and balanced way. The body needs a homeostatic or balanced way of functioning. Therefore, you must live in your body in a balanced way. It is both an intuitive and active way to allow yourself to be and to become who you are. You must give yourself permission to be in accord with your environment, your rhythm, and your aspirations. Your nervous system is very sensitive to your environment, and even if you think you are blocking certain things, you still are processing your reaction to your environment on a psychic and physiological level. However, being in accord with one's environment means to function appropriately in that environment. It does not mean necessarily being involved with everything that happens. Rather, it means to maintain one's center in the midst of all that happens.

Here is an example of the Law of Accord. A young man came to me with symptoms of periodic bouts of severe dizziness over a period of about four years. He had been to doctors and had been tested and nothing showed up. He had started attending college at the same time the symptoms of dizziness had begun. I saw immediately that the way he had been living his life was totally out of whack. He was living in such a frantic manner, it was as if he was constantly bashing himself against a brick wall. And an obvious symptom of bashing oneself against a brick wall is to be dizzy. So if he wanted his symptoms to go away he would have to choose to change his life accordingly.

The Law of Accord therefore demands that you live your life

with awareness, intuition and conscious caring for yourself. You cannot expect magic removal of symptoms that are there because your living in not balanced in the first place.

The Law of Kindness

Another spiritual law in healing that is included in the Law of Accord is the Law of Kindness. The Law of Kindness applies both to how you treat yourself and to how you treat each other. Although some people feel they should serve others and not themselves, service to yourself and each other is the same service. You cannot neglect yourself if you are to partake in the creative act of healing.

Most of us judge ourselves and each other very harshly; part of moving into the New Age means that we are relearning how to love ourselves unconditionally through all of the experiences and lessons life has to offer. Most people fight with themselves continually. The cells in their bodies react to this by becoming sick. The cells in your body react to whether you punish and fight with yourself. A disease like cancer is a manifestation of this self fighting. You must learn true gentleness and caring for yourself. Even if you make mistakes in life, or things don't go the way you plan, you must not continually punish yourself. You can take time and kindly talk to your body and tell it what you want to have healed. Here again, it is the bestowal of kindness to yourself that aids your cells in restoration. As you learn to be kind to yourself so you must learn to be kind to others. For if you hurt another person you are really hurting yourself and this can result in physical disease as well as mental or emotional discomfort. Being kind does not always mean being compliant with other people who are harmful to you. It is much deeper than that.

The Law of Forgiveness

We all tend to hang on to grudges and deep resentments of the past. Memories of the past really live within our cell structure; sometimes we are conscious of them and sometimes not. Due to these images of the past which lie both in our auric field and in the cells of our bodies we often carry around with us feelings of guilt and apprehension. Deep-seated resentment, against ourselves and others which we hold us from the hurts of the past acts upon our bodies and minds like the slow intake of poison. The only real way we can alleviate this feeling is to let go of resentment and forgive ourselves and whoever and whatever situation has hurt us. Energy of resentment that is kept inside of us is not healing energy. The way it can be transformed into healing energy is through forgiveness.

To release your resentment through forgiveness you go through a process. You let your pain surface. You can't reject your pain or hurt. You must accept them totally and offer them up as an act of Love to God. If you can not let go of your pain and anger, it is quite likely that you will be hurt again. You can actively pray to God to help you forgive and let go. You need to practice forgiveness of yourself and others continuously. It becomes constant prayer throughout your lives. By letting go you open to Grace. The Angels of Mercy are able to ease much sorrow of the past and comfort and protect you; you must help them out by actively seeking to forgive. You are the one who is your own worst enemy when withholding forgiveness of yourself and others.

One way you can forgive yourself is through repentance. Repentance is acknowledging that you've done an act that either violated yourself or another. We're all capable of hurting other people as well as ourselves and it is necessary to be able to let go of this consciously by acknowledging it. Repentance doesn't mean punishing yourself further, although in the Judeo-Christian and other traditions, such as Buddhism, a person can do a conscious act of repentance. Repentance basically means to acknowledge when you've done something wrong. It is asking forgiveness to the God within.

As well as the need to repent and forgive yourself for actual wrongs you've done either in thought or deed, you also have to forgive yourself for not loving yourself. There is not one transgression that you can perpetuate on another that you have not already perpetuated a thousand times on your own being. We judge ourselves so harshly it is unbelievable. It becomes a basic denial of the right to live. We must continually extend mercy to ourselves. This is our right and this is our duty.

One friend of mine on a plane trip wrote a love letter to herself:

Dear Marilyn,

You are wonderful! Your calm competence and incredible stamina today — and always — was amazingly impressive. In fact, you are an impressive woman and I am honored and pleasured to be associated with you.

You are beautiful! and I mean that! I know that for years you have felt frightened, unable to get, stay, in touch with your beauty and power, be in touch with your excellence. I appreciate your ability to let go of that, to grow into your full depth and stretch. To really, as the books say, become the best that you are. Self-Realized. A fully extended being. And I am grateful — and moved.

Your brilliance shines upon me like a beckoning light — to reach and grow and know that my hope shall be fulfilled. Amen.

I thank you. And all the wonderful people behind you — the moral, the spiritual, the financial, the hopeful supporters.

And I am grateful!

Amen. Alleluja.
God Bless!

The letter ended by Amen and Alleluja because by being loving to herself she was also participating in an act of praise to the holy one. Our cells vibrate in consciousness to a high joyful rhythm or vibration of love. When you don't allow yourself to delight in this love, your vitality falters and there is a greater chance for sickness to occur. When you can truly love yourself and one another, you can sing in accord with the Angels.

***Letter written by Marilyn Luco Sullivan**

The Law of Affirmation

The Law of Affirmation is basically the law of creative positive thinking. "As you think, so you shall be" is truer than most of us are consciously aware. To work with the Law of Affirmation is to continually affirm ourselves and the universe. It is a conscious rebuilding that is necessary in your healing process. The way you work with this Law is to affirm over to yourself many times a thought that is beneficial to us, such as "I am healthy" or "I am prosperous" or "I am good." You can affirm this thought by repeating it to yourself over and over, visualizing it, writing it down, making a sign and putting it in your room, or any other way you can imbibe it. You are actively nourishing yourself as you are doing this. It may well happen that your old buried or not so buried ideas of yourself surface to be released. It is best to see this process as a detoxification or as part of a healing crisis, and to offer these old thoughts to the Light of God. So working with the Law of Affirmation requires diligence, persistence and courage.

As you are able to give up fear and offer the old to the Light, you will be made new over and over again. This letting go and being made new is a dance in the rhythm of healing. In this giving up and opening to the Heart, the outpouring of the Spirit becomes a reality. This is the process of the opening of the Rose.

You can also think affirmative thoughts of other people. This is a powerful form of prayer and healing you can do for another and a way of blessing yourself by actively blessing another. A simple affirmation you can do for others is to affirm all good will come to the other and to mentally visualize the person surrounded by Light and Love. Another affirmation, or prayer to use for this Age is to visualize the planet filled and surrounded with Light.

Sometimes it is important to refuse illness or present conditions of unhappiness before you can affirm health. It is taking a stand of "No" before you can take a stand for "Yes". The most basic component in the Law of Affirmation is the fact that you have the right to exist. Without affirmation of your existence, no other affirmation can work. It is the negation of negation, the double negative of mathematics that yields a positive result. If, for instance, a person tells you that you cannot realize a goal you set for yourself, it is necessary to say "no" to that person's thought form.

CHAPTER IV
SUBTLE ENERGY IN HEALING

One of the basic premises of this book is that subtle energy affects grosser energy. The wave vibrational frequency is higher in subtle energy and can transmute grosser energy which has a slower frequency. Few of us are sensitive enough to see subtle energy with our physical eyes. But as we become more attuned to the Light, we become more attuned to subtle energy. Light and sound are the most subtle of all manifest energy. In the New Age the physician-priests will be working with Light, Color and Sound to heal the physical body. But in all of this work, the purity of heart is the most beautiful expression of subtle energy that there is.

Our bodies receive our thought impressions through the endocrine and nervous system. When we think and visualize ourselves healthy, it is the endocrine and nervous system which transmits this information to all of the systems in our body. When we think of ourselves as healthy our body receives the messages and acts on them accordingly. The pineal and pituitary glands play an important part of this functioning by controlling the messages that are relayed to the cells. The cells respond appropriately to the directives relayed. This is an example of the positive and negative feedback system.

If, for instance, you are eating too much fatty food in your diet, the circulation is affected and so you can't furnish yourself with nutrition or clear your wastes properly. Your cells communicate back to you that you need to eat less to stay healthy. The communication goes primarily through the endocrine system, but the nervous system also receives and transmits thought impressions directly. You should work creatively with thought by affirming health, while listening to the needs of our body.

The Aura In Healing

The physical body has a subtle field of energy around it called the Aura. The Auric field completely surrounds the body for two or three feet. Your emotions and thoughts are reflected in the aura as well as basic characteristics of your personality. Different colors and energy patterns in your Auric fields reflect inherent characteristics as well as present situations. You can feel your own Auric field by putting your hands facing each other about two feet apart and then moving them towards each other. At a subtle point you can begin to feel a pulsation between the two hands. This is where the Auric fields from each hand are meeting. It is a question of practice to teach your hands a fine sensitivity, so if you do not feel it the first time don't be discouraged. You are just beginning to learn to tune into a subtler vibration.

When you can feel the pulsating sensation between your hands, place your hands about three and a half feet around your head. Slowly move them towards your body until you once again feel a pulsating sensation.

The size and amount of radiance in a person's Auric field changes day to day depending on how a person is feeling. It is good to visualize your auric field as radiant and strong. Visualize Light around you sustaining, healing and protecting you. When your Auras are strong and filled with Light you are less susceptible to negative elements in your environment.

These negative elements can be chemical toxins, as well as people's thought forms. To visualize your Aura filled with Light means that you can stand strong in your own inner Light.

The Aura is very important in working with healing energy. The subtle energy of the Aura also takes in etheric vitamins from the elements of Air, Water, Earth and the Sun. These etheric vitamins help to make the physical body strong and vital through the Etheric Body, which is part of the Aura.

The Etheric Body is the part of the Aura which is closest to the body. It is often called the Golden Web because it looks like a golden web surrounding and interpenetrating the physical body at various points or matrices. The Etheric Body sustains the physical body. If there is a sudden shock to the physical body, it is important to visualize golden Light immediately around the Body maintaining the body. In working with the Etheric Body and the Aura, this clear force of visualization is very powerful.

A close friend of mine had a serious operation. When I tuned in physically to her condition after the operation, all I could see was these gases in her body. I concentrated on seeing her body strong and asked her guardian spirits to heal her through her subtle bodies. This helped in stabilizing her body condition, and she had a good recovery.

Even if you, or someone you know, is in good health, you can visualize your or their entire Auric field filled with Light and infusing your/their physical body with health and vitality.

The Earth also has an Etheric Body of Light which interpenetrates the earth at certain points. The more major of these intersections are power points on the Earth. An example of this, of course, is where the pyramids are built.

As well as visualizing Light filling the Auric field, you must understand that your thoughts and feelings are contained in your Auric field. This affects your health. For instance, if you have the thought form that you don't deserve to live, this will be transmitted from the Auric field through the Etheric Body to your physical body. What this means is that a certain part of the physical body will have devitalized energy and therefore is weakened and open to disease or disharmony. That is why it is so important that we think well of ourselves.

If you have negative thoughts and resentments towards others, this too will devitalize your physical body.

Your Auric fields are sensitive to other people's thought forms as well. If you keep company with people who are negatively minded, you are bound to feel the effects. If you keep company with people who generate love you are also bound to feel the effects. The more love you generate, the more love you attract to yourself.

Laying on of Hands

All of the poles of the body, the head, the hands and the feet, can pour out energy. In the practice of the Laying on of Hands, the healer is serving as a channel for the Healing Light to come through. It is as if the person who is the healer at that time is a transmitter for the Light. This helps to extend grace from the Kingdom of Heaven to the Earth. When I work with my hands in Healing, I first pray that I see the person who I am working with as a being of Love. I ask that I be made pure enough to perform this task and that I do not pick up any negativity that is released. I pray for the person who I am working with to be healed in the way that is the will of God. I then visualize the Light coming in the crown of my head and pouring out through my hands. Sometimes I place my hands directly on the person's body and at other times I place my hands on the person's Auric field. When I work with the person's Auric field I usually pick up thoughts which are restricting the person in some way. I can also pick up the degree the person is influenced by other people's thoughts. At the end of each healing, I visualize the Body and Aura strengthened and healed with the Light.

The act of Laying on of Hands is beautiful and simple. Used

with the power of the mind to visualize and communicate with the body it is a powerful mode of healing. It is good to tell the body to readjust itself at the same time.

Massage is really an adjunct to the Laying on of Hands. The body responds to subtle directives, and many wonderful results can be gained without pounding a person to death.

A friend's spine was slightly out of alignment. I put one finger lightly on the top of her spine where the neck and skull meet and told her spine to straighten itself. It did so immediately and she was relieved of the tension she had been feeling. Of course, in order for this to happen the person must be willing to want to be better.

CHAPTER V
MEMORIES IN HEALING

We must allow ourselves to be healed. We must allow the unchangeable Law of Love and Mercy to manifest in us. We are entitled to the Kingdom of Heaven.

The reasons for our sickness are implanted in our cells. A lot of these reasons we're not conscious of and I refer to them as our "shadow" in the sense that C.G. Jung used the term. That is the part of ourselves that is under the surface, or not acceptable to us. As we become aware of the "shadow" part and offer it to the Light, we can continue to be healed. When we are not aware of the "shadow" part of ourselves, we tend to act it out or express it through our mental and physical bodies. Sometimes this part of ourselves that is unacceptable is the part that holds rage and pain and anger, or is tender and vulnerable as a result of having been hurt.

Parental Memories

Sometimes this happens because we were conditioned by early childhood experiences or impressions. For instance, many of us thought we were not good as children, and so did not allow ourselves to feel good or to be well. Some of us made very subtle contracts with ourselves to be sick so we could be more acceptable to our parents. We needed love and approval from them in order to survive when we were very young, but many of us didn't receive this love and approval. So we thought that if we weren't well then perhaps we would receive the Love that we so desperately needed or we thought that if we got sick we would pay our parents back for not giving us the kind of Love we needed.

Finally we were allowed to be helpless, to be taken care of, and it was alright. We were acceptable and cared about. If we still have the need to be cared for, to be helpless, and to be loved, we can get sick. The way to deal with this again is to love ourselves, see the part of ourselves that needs to be taken care of, accept it totally and begin to really take care of ourselves. We need to rely on ourselves to see what our needs are and to make sure that they are met to the best of our abilities.

The memories of our past experiences and our thoughts and emotions from these experiences stored in the cells and tissues of our body need to be consciously reexperienced so that we can heal. A woman came to me with an infection of her fallopian tubes and uterus. When she was fifteen years old she became pregnant and decided to have the baby. Her parents sent her away and she stayed in a harsh home for unwed mothers and she had the labor all alone. She had a great deal of anger at her mother for deserting her at a time like that. Her parents suffered greatly throughout her pregnancy — her mother developed severe arthritis which only went away when the daughter was able to come home, and her parents were unable to have any sexual relationship during that period. Along with the anger and pain she felt towards her mother for leaving her was a deep-rooted feeling that she had done something wrong which was actually more damaging to her health than the pain and anger towards her family. This woman was actually discharging the memory through her current illness.

We must allow ourselves to look at the conditioning that tears away at our capacity to live, and breathe and be well. We must now allow ourselves to live in full acceptance and love of who we are, including the part of us that is vulnerable or is in pain.

Environmental and Experimental Memories

We also store the memories and effects of our early childhood environment with us. For some this could be a school environment or relationship to siblings. As already said, when we carry the memory of these events and impressions, often we continue to live them out through physical and emotional discomfort. Here is one example of this: I gave a consultation to a man who had an irritating skin condition for a good deal of his life, since the fifth grade. The skin condition was so bad that it kept people away from him. I saw and communicated to him that when he was an infant he was in a harsh environment that constantly irritated him. The atmosphere was barren of joy and his parents' moods were frequently harsh. He was not picked up very often and when he was, he was handled very roughly. He decided that this experience was his fault and he relegated himself to the position of an untouchable. Right here it is important to say that not only was his early environment harsh, but he also interpreted and reacted to it in a negative way, so really it is an interplay between events and impressions in our life as well as our reactions and interpretations of these events and impressions. This man's explanation for his unpleasant experience was that he was an untouchable, and so he continually relegated himself to this position by having the skin infection. In his life at the time of the consultation he didn't listen to his sensitivity and still picked up conditions which were harsh to him. He went to a therapist after the consultation and worked on his suppressed anger and pain about being treated harshly, and changed his living situtation to a kinder, more loving environment. Within four months his skin condition cleared up completely and has not returned since then.

Ancestral Memories

As well as having memories which are stored in our cells and Auras from early experience which affect us, we also have memories of ancestors which affect us. The memories of their impressions and attitudes have been passed down to us and sometimes we act out and experience these impressions.

I saw a thirty-four year old Irish-/American woman who firmly had the idea implanted in her that she was not going to get enough in life. She had that idea and was living it out. I could see an Irish woman dressed in black who was experiencing a famine in Ireland that was so severe that babies stomachs were turning black from starvation. This woman carried this memory with her although she was unaware of it. In a case similar to this, it would be good to work with affirmation. Perhaps by saying simply, "I will have what I need in my life."

All of our experiences, including our impressions of our parents, siblings and relatives, and our reaction to our day to day living situations can be sources of beauty and strength. It is important to turn all experience to our advantage. It is necessary for us to give thanks and appreciate, all of our life experience. This opening in thankfulness to all of our circumstances whether they were painful or pleasurable is the key to the gateway of heaven. It enables us to receive the good and love in bounty and at the same time it enables us to achieve equanimity in adversity without blaming ourselves or each other and suffering from this blame. We must attain enough spiritual insight to understand that all that is given is given in grace. The more we can be thankful, the more loving we can be, the more we can receive the grace.

We come into this life with Karma from past lives, too. Karma is very mysterious; it is the law of cause and effect in the universe. Once a friend's child was going through a lot of turmoil with a man who was in the role of his step-father. I held him on my lap and as he began to relax I could see a past life in England where he and the person he was involved with currently were fighting. I then saw these highly evolved beings who were the lords of Karma. They gave him grace and he slept for a few minutes and woke up in a wonderful mood. So it became clear that it was his Karma which created the situation in the first place. It no longer does any good to blame someone else when it is our own Karma which creates these situations to begin with.

Some people who came to me for consultations want very much to go into their past lives. I don't encourage this unless it is somehow relevant to what they are currently dealing with; we've had countless past lives and our minds are already so cluttered up from them.

But occasionally it arises and here is an example of one occasion. A woman came to see me who was doing relatively high pressured work yet at the same time she was experiencing a lot of insecurity about her functioning. As we began the consultation we both saw her wearing a gown with a hood and a protective shield. There were lots of people on both sides of her who wanted something from her. We both immediately had a sense of her being in ancient Egypt. She went on to see that her role was to bring justice to people; with her right hand she could give mercy and with her left hand punishment. Then she kept saying, "There is something I'm doing wrong." I encouraged her to find out what it was that she was doing and she saw herself giving punishment to someone who didn't deserve the punishment. She gave out more punishment than mercy. I then asked her to ask for forgiveness from God, which she did by silently going inside. The forgiveness was immediately given. By the end of the session her shoulders, which were originally slumped over, straightened up, and she looked like a different person than when she came in. Now she could mentally wear the protective shield of Light without fearing the corruption.

Another man I saw was in an English prison cell in the late Middle Ages where there was only one window in the room high above him which let the Light in. He refused to see the Light but kept looking around at this miserly conditions. To this day he was still in part refusing to look at the Light and needed to hear that to help release his negative attitude.

It is not necessary to remember past lives to overcome our mental and physical limitations. What is necessary is to always turn towards the Light within ourselves.

Again, it is important to be kind to ourselves and to those around us in our process. All of the memories of the past cannot free us from our suffering as much as can one minute of genuine kindness to ourselves.

As well as recognizing and letting go of memories of the past we must also engage in the active act of remembrance of who we really are. We are all beings of the Light of God and to think less of ourselves fills us with restlessness. To hold in our mind the remembrance of our true heritage is to move into the Kingdom of Light and Truth. Through regular, repeated remembrance we acquire our birthright.

CHAPTER VI

ASPECTS OF OUR COLLECTIVE HEALING

We are being healed together. Our group consciousness is shifting to a higher, lighter vibration. As we shift to a purer level of consciousness we experience surfacing of our negativities. It is as if we are all involved in a healing crisis at least some of the time. This surfacing of our negativities is a cleansing. We must not permit ourselves to be discouraged in these times. We must continue to turn towards the Light. In each turning we are able to let go more of what we are not As we continue to turn towards the Light we turn towards each other as true brothers and sisters in the body of the Holy One. This is the plan for our planet. This is the plan for our soul's evolution.

When I've done work with groups of people, certain life-denying thought forms keep surfacing. One is, "I'm no good," or "I'm not good enough," This thought form gives rise to lots of illness and mental and emotional discomfort.

A thought form of similar effect is, "I don't deserve to live," and another one is "I'm not worthy to receive love." All of these thought-forms have been transmitted from one generation to the next and so we are in effect inheritors.

To counterbalance this effect we must take a stand for ourselves and each other and affirm "I am good enough," "I deserve to live," "I am worthy of great happiness."

We deserve the right to experience the beauty of the story of our life without constantly negating ourselves. One way we subtly negate ourselves is by carrying around expectations. We think we are not doing something right or the situation isn't right. We have so much difficulty just giving ourselves permission to be alive. We expect so much from others, and often experience great pain that is truly unnecessary. We are wonderful beings who have the gateway of heaven accessible to us right within us.

We live in a great amount of fear that we will not have enough. Part of this fear is a group ancestral memory and part of it is because we do not think we have what we need.

We need to see the portals of heaven open to us, and we need to receive with joy the love that is in our lives. We need to accept the goodness and bounty of the Universe which is limitless love. Once we begin to accept the Love and Grace that is so freely bestowed upon us, we can receive the bounty of the Universe. Many of us still carry around expectations that things will not work out well. And so they do not. Here again is the Law of Attraction. Whatever we attract to ourselves is what we invite by our own thoughts and feelings. Now is the time to accept that things will work out well for us and for the planet. As well as accepting the goodness of the Universe, we have to realize that that Universe is within. Meditation is the way to discover that. And we understand more fully that we are the Light and Love we can more fully give to each other as brothers and sisters. This will enable us to experience more and so our inner experience and outer worlds merge in Love. This is where we are headed.

We all suffer the discomfort of being easily influenced by other people's opinions. We feel that if people approve of us we are proved worthwhile. If we meet with disapproval or negativity we react physically. I recently saw a woman who had hepatitis, a disease of the liver. I did a consultaion with her and saw that she absorbed people's negtive thoughts. If a person didn't like something about her she immediately assumed the person was correct. She even attracted negative thoughts to her that had nothing to do with her. Her parents in her early childhood were very critical of her, so she was used to absorbing that kind of negativity. It was, in fact, the accepted pattern in her life. Before she got the hepatitis she experienced a very upsetting incident where one of the leaders in her community didn't want her to be part of the community. She was so influenced by his thoughts that it contributed to her illness. She didn't want to live if someone was critical of her. The affirmation that she worked with was, "My survival is dependent on the creative spirit of God."

If you have a strong and radiant Auric field, it is less likely that you will be influenced by other people's thoughts. The true cause of a strong Auric field is being at ease and accepting that we are the source of our well-being. This is not something that happens automatically, but requires effort and patience. Part of this effort is being discriminating in the company you keep. If you are with people who have love for God in their hearts, for themselves and for other people, it is so much easier to feel good about yourself. Meeting with people who are like-minded in this respect and doing spiritual work, prayer and meditation is tremendously nourishing.

It is food for us. What we give ourselves to nourish ourselves is not only physical food but spiritual food as well.

There are times in our day when we cannot control our environment. A way to strengthen our being during these times is to visualize ourselves totally encased in Light. This Light is so powerful that it will only permit us to receive that is helpful to us. We can also visualize our loved ones surrounded by Light and protection. This form of visualization works over distances. The Aura actually is a body of Light, so as we visualize ourselves surrounded with Light we become closer attuned to the Light.

As the New Age approaches we are drawn inexorably towards the Light. We must leave behind expectations that we have of ourselves and others. We all carry the burden of expecting ourselves to be some other way. This is a basic act of non-acceptance of the right to be. We are so beautiful just the way we are. We deserve to live by the mere fact that we are grace. We are not defined by our immediate situation. We are beautiful because we are the love of the Lord. We experience mercy when we allow ourselves to trust our experience. We experience grace when we allow ourselves to be without putting qualifications on our existence. We suffer needlessly when we do not allow ourselves to be. We suffer needlessly when we shut out the Love and grace and total support of the universe.

It is the time of gathering together to strengthen our kinship and common purpose. Let us do this in the spirit of celebration. Let us join together and send our prayers to the entire planet and the leaders of the planet so that the Earth can move to her new vibration of Light. Let us gather together with the purity of our hearts and overcome our differences. It is the time for reconciliation. Let us strengthen and encourage each other in our endeavors. Let us weep no more. Let us overcome our impurity by knowing our purity. The cleansing has begun. Let us be born anew within each other's hearts.

Acknowledgements:

1) *Swami Muktananda Paramahansa*
2) *Sri Bhagavad Nityananda*
3) *Jesus and Mary*
4) *New York Siddha Yoga Dham*
5) *Karmu*
6) *The folks in Amherst, Mass.*
7) *Maggie Barritt*

BIBLIOGRAPHY

Be Well; Mike Samuels and Hal Bennett, Random House/Bookworks, New York, 1974.

The Well Body Book; Mike Samuels and Hal Bennett, Random House/Bookworks.

The Healing of Secret Ages; Catherine Ponder, Parker Publishing Co., W. Nyack, N.Y.

Revelation, The Birth of a New Age; David Spangler, Rainbow Bridge.

The Ministry of Angels, Here and Beyond; Joy Snell, Citadel Press, Secaucus, N.J., 1977.

Thought Power; Swami Sivananda, Divine Life Society.

The Power of the Rays, The Science of Color Healing; S.G.J. Ouseley, L.N. Fowler & Co., Ltd., 15 New Bridge St., London, EC4V6BB England.

Play of Consciousness; Swami Muktananda Paramahansa, Shree Gurudev Siddha Yoga Ashram, 1974.

Development of Spiritual Healing; Hazrat Inayat Khan, Sufi Publishing Co. Ltd., U.K.